THE MAN WHO SAW THE DEVIL

Borgo Press Books Translated by FRANK J. MORLOCK

THE MAN WHO SAW THE DEVIL

A PLAY IN TWO ACTS

by

GASTON LEROUX

Adapted and Translated by Frank J. Morlock

THE BORGO PRESS

An Imprint of Wildside Press LLC

MMIX

www.wildsidebooks.com

FIRST WILDSIDE EDITION

CONTENTS

DEDICATION

TO JOHN GREGORY BETANCOURT,

WHO WILL APPRECIATE THIS

CAST OF CHARACTERS

THE MAN, Nice-looking old man of eighty

ALLAN, around thirty-five, simple elegance, dressed in hunting costume

THE OTHER, who resembles ALLAN like a brother

MATHIS, A rich proprietor from the Jura mountains, in hunting costume, of brutal and dull appearance

MATHIEU

GUILLAUME, the Man's servant, around thirty-five

CLAIRELI, the young wife of Mathis, not at all provincial, in hunting costume, forceful and shrewd

MAMA APPENZEL, almost as old as The

Man, whose active servant she is

ACT I

Both acts use the same set. An old dining room for gentlemen. Large beams in the ceiling. An immense hearth at the back. Door on the left giving on the mountain. By the door on the left a window with closed shutters. To the right near the audience, a small wooden stairway which climbs to a door leading to the Man's room. At the rear, to the right of the chimney, another door leading into the apartments. To the left, at the back, in cutaway, a strangely formed door decorated with a large painted cross. Square table, a large armchair near the hearth. Chairs, torches. To the right, against the wall, a dresser. Old, simple furniture, a bit lugubrious, but nothing fantastic except the door with the cross.

At rise, it is evening. Everything is locked up because the weather is frightful and the wind is shaking the old building to its foundations. The room is lit only by the fire in the hearth. Knocking is heard at the door and voices in tumult outside.

MAMA:
(looking towards the door scornfully) Who is knocking at such an hour?

(she cautiously approaches the door) Who is there?

VOICES OUTSIDE:
Open! Open fast!

MATHIEU:
Someone's injured.

MAMA:
Injured?

(She pulls back the bolt and opens the door. Mathieu and Claireli burst in. Allan, supporting Mathis, comes behind. The newcomers are outfitted as hunters, rifles in bandoleros. Mathis is all white, like someone who had rolled in the snow. He alone has no rifle.)

CLAIRELI:
Well, old woman, it's not too soon!

MATHIEU:
(taking a rifle from his bandolero and that of Mathis in his hand) Did you want to let us croak outside?

MAMA:
(after having looked at the door and looking at Mathis) So what happened to you?

MATHIS:
(drinking a bit) More fright than harm! Luckily!

ALLAN:
A misstep. He rolled in the snow.

MATHIEU:

In the snow? In the precipice, yes! Ah! My poor old friend! — I still haven't got over it completely!

CLAIRELI:

(placing her rifle) Whew! It's nice here —

ALLAN:

(to Mathis) Now there's a nice fire! Sit down!

(Mathis sits and Allan goes to rid himself quickly of his game bag which he deposits in a corner at the right, quite near the wooden stairway; doing so, he speaks to Mathis) But get hold of yourself, sonofabitch — You are still trembling!

MATHIS:

Ah! I had one hell of a scare!

MATHIEU:

(relieving himself of his weapons and game bags to the right of where Allan deposited his) As for me, I thought that was it.

MATHIS:
For sure, that was it. There was no mistake about it. If Allan hadn't been there at the exact moment to offer me his hand — when I think about it.

(Mathis looks at Allan with gratitude.)

ALLAN:
Hey! — don't think about it and dry yourself off.

(A pause.)

MATHIS:
Well, Claireli, you aren't saying anything! You just missed being a widow, you know —

CLAIRELI:
(gravely) It's true, Allan! You saved the life of my husband!

ALLAN:
Leave me in peace.

MATHIS:
(half joking to Claireli) Do you regret it?

CLAIRELI:
I see you are better, Mathis! You are joking.

MATHIS:
(looking at them all) Yes, now I want to laugh — Ah! My old friend!

MAMA:
I bet it happened on the side of the Grande Marnière — That area is treacherous! Little Leduc found death there last year.

MATHIEU:
Aren't we facing Grande Marnière? I thought that when you turned your back.

MAMA:
Ah, that's the way it is, you were lost on the mountain.

MATHIEU:
There are some circumstances, with the af-

ternoon fog, and then the storm that came up at night.

CLAIRELI:
Yes, luckily we noticed the light.

MAMA:
Eh! You must be very worn out, my little lady. Come on, rest, I am going to heat you up something.

(Mama brings up a chair.)

ALLAN:
(rising and going to Claireli) It's true, Claireli — no one is taking care of you.

CLAIRELI:
Thanks, Allan, but look after my husband.

(Allan looks at Claireli without responding.)

MATHIEU:
What nasty weather! Who is it would have thought it? Ah! The mountain! You never can

tell about it.

(claps Mathis, who is quite pensive by the fire, on the back) Well, my old friend, are you yourself again? Your leg —

MATHIS:
(rising, making his leg stretch and move about) Oh! Completely okay. I am just a bit shocked, that's all.

(Meanwhile, the old woman is placing serving settings on the table, after taking them from the dresser.)

MATHIEU:
Can we sleep here? Where are we here?

MAMA:
(jogging around to the stairs as if the question had made her flee) At the home of brave folks, my dear sir, who won't let you die of cold or hunger, I am going to inform my master.

(Mama clambers up the stairway.)

ALLAN:
Go, my brave woman, go! And return quickly with a fine soup. As for me, I'm starving.

MATHIS:
(who's turned and is examining the place, says suddenly, in a hesitant, slightly frightened voice as he looks at the cross) Indeed! Ah! Why? —

ALLAN:
What?

CLAIRELI:
(to Allan, looking at Mathis) What's got him?

MATHIS:
(who has taken a few steps toward the door with the cross, and who stops, more and more frightened) Why, it's the door of the cross!

MATHIEU:
(turning abruptly) The door of the cross!

MATHIS:
(recoiling) We are at the man's home!

MATHIEU:
(taking a step to the door of the cross, brutally) Why, indeed — it's certain! Ah! I ought to have suspected it myself! But I thought you had to be turning your back to Grande Marnière.

ALLAN:
But in the end, we are at his place.

MATHIS:
(more and more agitated) Eh! At the home of the man who has seen the devil.

ALLAN:
Huh?

CLAIRELI:
(shrugging her shoulders) Mountain legends.

MATHIS:
There's only one door like this on the whole

mountain.

(to the old woman who has stopped on the stairway) What's that door there?

MAMA:
That's nothing!

MATHIEU:
Why's there a big cross on it?

MAMA:
For nothing.

MATHIS:
But where's this door lead?

MAMA:
Nowhere!

(she leaves)

ALLAN:
(going to touch the door) Still, what's the legend about?

MATHIEU:
(brutally holding Allan's arm) Don't touch that door!

MATHIS:
(by the window) You are right, we mustn't touch anything here, nothing! We must leave.

CLAIRELI:
(hostile) Leave!

ALLAN:
Leave!

MATHIEU:
Yes — the house brings bad luck! Little Leduc, for having only rapped on this door in terror, one stormy night like this one, was found the next day at the bottom of Grande Marnière.

ALLAN:
You make me laugh. If Little Leduc had remained here, he wouldn't be dead.

MATHIS:
What do you know about it? If I tell you that I prefer to be facing precipices than to remain in this house?

ALLAN:
Why?

MATHIEU:
Eh! Because it's that man's house.

MATHIS:
Not for any other reason?

ALLAN:
(going to Claireli) Why, they are linked together in madness.

CLAIRELI:
(in the depth of her chair warming her feet) They ought to be locked up! You will see, they will end by locking the two of them up with their old wives tales.

MATHIS:
Don't laugh. From what it appears, it's true. All the more true.

MATHIEU:
There was a proof given — a few years ago.

ALLAN:
What proof?

MATHIS:
The man will tell you, perhaps, if you stay around here! As for us, trust me —

(Mathis gestures to depart, gets his rifle, and returns to the table.)

ALLAN:
No! seriously — you want to leave? Listen to the wind. The whole mountain is shaken to its base.

CLAIRELI:
Now that's enough! We will spend the night here.

(to Mathis) Now, if it pleases you to descend to La Chaux de Fonds on the paths he takes, goodnight!

ALLAN:
This is too stupid! Let them leave.

MATHIS:
That's good — that's fine — You asked for it — What will happen, will happen! Let the will of Claireli be accomplished!

(Mathis places his rifle back; Mathieu does the same.)

MATHIEU:
We're making a mistake; you will see that we've made a mistake!

(Mama Appenzel appears at the top of the stairway.)

MAMA:
The master sends you his compliments — But come, before supper, I am going to show

you to your rooms.

(she opens the door at the back) Ah! There you are in front of that door! If he saw you, he would be very angry.

ALLAN:
What's this all about?

MAMA:
It's a story that doesn't concern anybody —

(Mama leaves with Mathieu and Allan. Mathieu has taken his rifle.)

MATHIS:
(to Claireli, pointing to the door with the cross) You think it's natural to have that cross on that door?

CLAIRELI:
(unnerved) I assure you, Mathis, that there are moments when I think you are stupid!

MATHIS:
Yes, I've noticed there are moments like that!

CLAIRELI:
You are exasperating me, in the end, with your mania to vex everybody. You will make yourself unbearable to your best friends. Allan doesn't come to see us so often!

MATHIS:
(somberly) Allan is an old comrade of mine, a childhood companion, a friend — a true friend — and I really believe that, just now, he saved my life. It's true he only did what anyone would have done in his place — Well! — If he no longer comes to see us! (a pause) I will console myself about it.

CLAIRELI:
Ah!

MATHIS:
Yes, I've noticed it's when he's around that you find me stupid —

(Mathis leaves.)

MATHIEU:
(in the wings) Mathis, are you coming? What is it you are doing?

(Claireli looks at Mathis with hate as he leaves. She leans on her elbows, with despair, on the arms of the armchair, staring at the fireplace without seeing anything.)

ALLAN:
(appearing at the door Mathis went out) Well, aren't you coming to your room?

MATHIS:
(in the hallway) Yes, yes —

CLAIRELI:
You know that he is jealous now?

ALLAN:
Yes, — His friend is keeping an eye on us!

CLAIRELI:

Allan! Allan! Allan! — (she extends her arms towards him) My Allan!

ALLAN:

(taking her in his arms, lovingly) Claireli!

CLAIRELI:

(in tears) Ah! To live between those two brutes! I no longer want to see them — never to see them —

ALLAN:

(uneasily) Claireli — I beg you.

CLAIRELI:

As for you, how calm you are! And what cool blood! Without cool blood just now — yes, you understand well enough what I mean — don't turn your eyes away — Without you, he would be —

(she makes a sign of falling) You saved him.

ALLAN:
That's true!

CLAIRELI:
Why did you do that?

ALLAN:
(going towards her) Claireli! Claireli! — You
frighten me!

CLAIRELI:
(holding him back) Dare to say for once what
you have often thought — I've seen your
eyes, sometimes, when he was kissing me.

ALLAN:
Oh! Claireli —

CLAIRELI:
If your eyes had been pistols —

ALLAN:
That's true. But that's the crime of all jealous
lovers. Luckily, their eyes do not kill.

CLAIRELI:
(with an almost savage bitterness) You are an honest man, Allan! All my compliments! But as for me — me, what is it I am? What is it you have made of me? What will I become when you are going to leave? I, who can no longer do without you! Do you know what he said to me just now? That he will take consolation from no longer seeing you. I tell you that he suspects something, he and his friend. Allan! I tell you, you do not love me!

ALLAN:
Shut up! Shut up! You know very well that I am mad about you.

CLAIRELI:
(looking in his eyes) You are lying — if you really wanted — if you really wanted —

(Allan's back is to the public; she speaks, lovingly) Coward!

(They go silent momentarily, eyes on eyes.)

MATHIS:
(coming in from the door at the back) There are only two rooms.

ALLAN:
That will suffice; as for me, I will spend the night here.

CLAIRELI:
If we were all to spend the night here — We could make a party. Mathis has cards.

MAN:
(entering at the top of the stairway) Good evening, my guests!

(he comes down calmly with a very grand air. He's dressed in antique clothes, shoes, silk stockings with buckles, elegant like Beau Brummel. He bows very naturally to Claireli) You must be very tired, madame, and you are going to find impoverished hospitality here.

CLAIRELI:
Oh, sir! We are the ones who do not know

how to make excuses for ourselves.

MAN:
For what, madame? For having brought much grace into my little abode?

ALLAN:
(aside) Why, he's very fine, this old Satan!

(aloud) Dear host, will you permit us to introduce ourselves?

(as Mama Appenzel finishes laying the table) Madame Mathis Brunner, and my friend Brunner, a real Swiss from the old cantons, installed for some years in your country; our friend Mathieu; two old comrades from the college of your servant, Allan Danglade, head of the clinic at the faculty of Nancy.

MAN:
(inviting his guests to sit) Madame — Gentlemen.

(sitting) What was my old servant telling me?

You've had an accident?

(All are seated around the table; Mathis and Mathieu display a certain hesitancy.)

CLAIRELI:
We almost had an accident — yes, my husband slipped — but fortunately we got off with a fright.

(Mama Appenzel brings the soup bowl to the table.)

MAN:
(to Claireli) The mountain is really dangerous because of this abominable weather. Madame, you will allow me to serve you myself? A cabbage soup — a peasant soup?

CLAIRELI:
It smells like perfume.

MAN:
(after having served Claireli) Serve these gentlemen, mother. And then, you are going

to find us a bottle of my old Neufchatel. You are worn out, surprised by the storm?

CLAIRELI:
The weather was so fine this morning!

MAN:
What! You've hunted since morning! You are fearless!

ALLAN:
Fearless! It's due to Madame Brunner that we wandered far from where we were thinking of.

CLAIRELI:
And because of you, dear friend, that we are returning empty handed. You completely lack coolness — it's unforgivable in a doctor.

ALLAN:
It's true, I am very nervous.

CLAIRELI:
And very clumsy.

ALLAN:
(to the Man) She's mean! But I am accustomed to it. My friends are always kidding me about my awkwardness.

CLAIRELI:
When he sees the stag — he doesn't know which end of the rifle to take!

MAN:
That's very dangerous.

MATHIS:
(deciding to place a churlish word in) And then he always leaves his gun sights at the house.

ALLAN:
(eating) There it is — I was expecting that! "He always forgets his gun sights at the house" — What do you want? I didn't learn to shoot at Chamois in the course of medical school. — You know, your soup is famous.

(Mathis and Mathieu don't touch their

bowls.)

MAN:
(serving wine) And my Neufchatel?

ALLAN:
Admirable — a delightful flavor.

(to Mathis and Mathieu) Well, sons of William Tell, you are not eating! I propose the health of our host.

MAN:
(raising his glass) To your health, madame.

(After having drunk, to Mathis and Mathieu) These gentlemen haven't taken anything?

MATHIS:
I'm not hungry.

MATHIEU:
Me, either.

MAN:
(sadly) An excess of fatigue, no doubt. You've seen your rooms? Unfortunately, I can dispose of only two beds.

ALLAN:
If it doesn't disturb you, sir, my friends and I have decided to spend the night here in this room.

MAN:
(astonished) Not at all — but Madame Brunner must need some rest.

(The wind increases its force.)

CLAIRELI:
How to sleep in this storm!

(to the Man) And then, these gentlemen have put together a little project.

(Claireli smiles at Allan.)

MAN:
What project, madame?

CLAIRELI:
That of spending the night playing cards. It won't be the first.

MAN:
(in a dull voice) Gambling!

(after a silence) You gamble, madame?

CLAIRELI:
Indeed, yes. And you? You don't like gambling?

MAN:
(somberly) No — and there's nothing here to play with!

ALLAN:
We have cards!

MAN:
(rising slowly) You came with cards?

(to the others who rise) Stay put — stay put! You are at home here.

(a silence) Go ahead, play!

CLAIRELI:
We've vexed you.

MAN:
No! No!

CLAIRELI:
Yes! Yes!

MAN:
I assure you, madame.

CLAIRELI:
Ah, I see it plainly. As soon as we spoke of cards — Eh! We won't play.

MAN:
(protesting politely) Oh! Madame!

CLAIRELI:
In any case, we are not in a hurry. We won't leave like this.

(with a gracious gesture) Sit down!

MAN:
(who has sat back in obedience to Claireli's gracious gesture) I ask your pardon.

CLAIRELI:
(threatening him with a finger) As for you, our host, you must be a terrible gambler.

MAN:
(very gravely) You said the word, madame, terrible —

ALLAN:
And you've lost at gambling, like everybody else?

MAN:
(icily) More than everybody else, doctor — I lost my soul to it.

ALLAN:
Your soul?

MAN:
You don't believe in the soul?

ALLAN:
That's an embarrassing question — even for a professional of the faculty of Nancy.

MAN:
Yes, there was a time when, I no more believed in God nor in—

CLAIRELI:
Nor in what?

MAN:
Why are you looking at me this way?

CLAIRELI:
You perhaps suspect that —

MAN:
And I do not frighten you?

CLAIRELI:
You intrigue me.

MAN:
It doesn't make you uneasy to find yourself, this evening — in my abode?

CLAIRELI:
No! Why?

MAN:
Ask these gentlemen who haven't touched a crumb of my bread! Not a drop of my wine! They know very well, they do, that my house brings misfortune!

ALLAN:
(touching his face with his finger as he looks at the Man) Now there we are! I am convinced that there are crazies in this country. There are those who say that you saw the devil!

MAN:
(icily) Truly!

CLAIRELI:
The way you say that!

MATHIS:
(brutally and with terror) You shut up, you hear. That's enough of that! What the gentleman has seen or hasn't seen is his affair — it's no concern of ours!

CLAIRELI:
You are going nuts, Mathis — we were talking —

MATHIS:
(brutal) You do not talk about things like that.

(the wind, the storm increase) Ah! This storm!

MAN:
(somberly) Yes, there hasn't been one like it — for very many years.

CLAIRELI:
It's true that the wind, this evening — is in abominable voice.

MAMA:
(entering with the service) You'd say a dog was howling at death!

MAN:
(to the old woman) Shut up! You know quite well that I've forbidden you to utter that word here.

(he looks at her in wrath and she vanishes under the stairway) I ask your pardon — I cannot hear that word pronounced. You, you don't know what it is; you are young — but as for me — I have so much fear of death that I'd prefer to be dead so as to no longer be afraid of it.

ALLAN:
I've seen people who killed themselves because they were afraid of dying.

CLAIRELI:
No?

MAN:
Don't smile — I understand that! Ah! It's a frightful thing you see — to leave! When you know he's waiting for you and that he's concerned only about you and that he's there perhaps, already, behind the window, behind the shed — expecting you.

(Sinister howling of the wind.)

CLAIRELI:
(very entranced) Then — it's true what they say? You have seen him — the Devil?

MAN:
(rising) Just as I see you, madame!

(All rise. Mathieu and Mathis recoil, frightened.)

ALLAN:
(jesting) That cost you dearly?

MAN:
(extending his arms) The whole fortune of the world!

ALLAN:
Truly?

MAN:
(with a gesture looking at Allan) You don't believe me?

ALLAN:
My word, no!

MAN:
(somberly, hesitating) And if it were proved to you?

ALLAN:
(laughing) You were dreaming.

MAN:
Yes, naturally, you doubt it, you, the man of science —

ALLAN:
(conciliatory) Ah, science — You know, my dear host —

MAN:
You don't believe it, either. In what do you believe then?

ALLAN:
Difficult — difficult to say —

MAN:
Meanwhile, you jest.

ALLAN:
No indeed! I don't even know what it's about.

MAN:
Well, I am going to tell you — You were speaking of gambling, just now. I ruined myself at it — millions devoured.

(The Man stops abruptly in his narration. A pause.)

CLAIRELI:
(insinuating) Then?

MAN:
At that period, I was ruined and in love! Yes, I loved a very rich young girl like a madman! That henceforth I had to renounce.

(a pause) In short, one evening, in my distress, I found myself in this old manor — all that remained to me of my family property. Everything happened the first evening.

(a long pause) I was in this place, my rifle loaded, awaiting my last will in that corner exactly where you find (pointing to the corner where Allan has placed his rifle) that one.

ALLAN:
Mine!

MAN:
Ah! Suddenly the calm succeeded the unleashing of the storm. I opened the window: the first thing that I saw was a large mo-

tionless vulture above la Roche-plate, and quite black against the moon. This lugubrious bird set me on edge with its fixed way of staring at me. I shot at it — almost point blank — and I am a good shot. It didn't even budge — and it continued to stare at me in a sneering, sinister manner. I left the window and I set myself to writing, at this table, at this spot, my last letter to my fiancée, when, having raised my head, I saw facing me, there! (rising and pointing to the door) there, where I've since placed a door with a cross — and where at the time was found a large mirror — I saw the mirror move and turn. I rose, intrigued. The mirror used to be the door to a cupboard: what could be more simple? Its own weight had caused it to turn in, that was all! I looked in the cupboard. I found some old works which dealt with sorcery. One of them, entitled *The Sorcerer of the Jura*, quickly attracted my attention — because on the cover was imprinted a great, black vulture, just like the one I had just missed that very moment.

(to Allan) Oh! That doesn't prove anything — but wait! I opened this book; the first two lines made my eyes pop out. They said: "When one sincerely wishes to see the devil, all you need to do is call him, he will come! But you must call him with all your heart." I threw the book into the cupboard and re-placed the mirror. My pallor was so great I thought I was face to face with a cadaver! Alas! No, the man in front of this mirror was not dead! But a living person who evoked the king of the dead! Yes, I did that, I did, who never thought about anything. With all my heart, I called him to my assistance, to my as-sistance! And suddenly the face in the mirror spoke. It said to me: "Here I am! But I'm locked in here — open this door — will you open it?" And as I didn't dare, he struck three times on the door of the armoire — and the door opened all by itself.

(At this moment three knocks are distinctly heard at the entrance door. All, entranced, look toward the entrance door, and the gen-tleman recoils instinctively seeing the door which seems to open by itself, slowly, pushed from without. At last, opened, it reveals on the sill a person covered with a cloak, his face hidden by a hat which he clutches, motionless.)

MAN:
(rudely) Who is there? Ah! It's you, Guillaume? Well — come in.

GUILLAUME:
(sitting down with hesitation and removing his hat) I didn't know that you had company — I wouldn't have pushed the door.

MAN:
You've seen the notary?

(to the others) I beg your pardon, gentlemen — my servant, the grandson of the old woman who was serving you just now.

GUILLAUME:
(pulling a sack from under his cloak, and removing papers and envelopes from it) Here

are the papers (putting them on the table), and here's the payment for the wood from Misère.

(he takes bills from the envelope and counts to ten) Ten thousand — the account is there.

MAN:
(counting in his turn, replacing the money in the envelope and leaving the envelope on the table) That's fine. Are you hungry?

GUILLAUME:
No, I broke a crust on route.

MAN:
(reading his papers) Then go rest, you must be tired.

GUILLAUME:
I have to sleep at the farmer's. I have business with him early.

MAN:
I need to see you tomorrow morning.

GUILLAUME:
Oh! I will be back early.

MAN:
Well, take your papers back — we will look at them together.

(he pulls a billfold from his pocket and puts the envelope in his billfold) Ten thousand — the wood at Misère — What did the notary say to you?

(The Man replaces the billfold in his pocket.)

GUILLAUME:
(picking up the papers and placing them in his bag) That it was for nothing!

(going towards the door)

MAN:
Mother and I, we were no longer expecting you in such weather.

GUILLAUME:
Ah! I will come in any weather. I didn't want to keep that money on me. Goodnight!

MAN:
Goodnight, Guillaume!

(Guillaume leaves.)

CLAIRELI:
(as the Man places the bolt in the door) And afterwards?

ALLAN:
After the door to the cupboard opened by it-self?

CLAIRELI:
What was in the cupboard?

MAN:
There was something which burned my eyes — in letters of fire — (exultantly) Three words. "You will win!"

ALLAN:
What do you mean? "You will win!"

MAN:
(brutally) You don't get it? In three words, in the depth of the armoire, the devil wrote my destiny in burning letters! "You will win!" Ruined gambler, I wanted to become rich again, and he told me simply: "You will win!" In three words he gave me the wealth of the whole world. You will win! Now do you understand?

ALLAN:
Yes, indeed! And I know gamblers who would indeed like to meet that devil.

MAN:
Ah, I beseech you, don't joke anymore. The next day, Mama Appenzel found me curled up at the foot of the cupboard. After they revived me, alas! I hadn't forgotten a thing! I must never forget.

ALLAN:
And you won?

MAN:
(with frightening somberness) Always!

ALLAN:
What do you mean — always?

MAN:
Yes, indeed: always!

ALLAN:
Indeed, for goodness sake.

MAN:
(abruptly) Do you think I am lying?

ALLAN:
No! But I think you were the victim of an hallucination.

MAN:
(on edge) Yes, I know! You don't need to be a scientist to have such an idea! I had it, that

idea. I borrowed some money on this house, a few days later at my club, I put in an appearance saying: "We are going to see this time, if the devil assisting—" I hadn't finished my phrase. They set the bank high when I entered the room. I took it for two hundred crowns. I hadn't reached the middle of the cut when I won three hundred thousand francs. Only they couldn't punt against me. Yes, I'd terrified the punt, because I won every round. I was amusing myself then, to win points for nothing, to see, for the pleasure. I lost every point — on those which no one bet money against me, which underlined my luck!

CLAIRELI:
And then?

MAN:
I wanted to have a pure heart! I set myself to gambling; when I left the club at six in the morning, I had made money each time.

CLAIRELI:
You didn't lose a bet!

MAN:
Not one!

CLAIRELI:
What do you say to that, Allan?

ALLAN:
(rising and going to the chimney) I say that I'd really like to play with the gentleman.

MATHIS, MATHIEU:
(low voice, rapidly) No indeed, Allan, it's useless.

ALLAN:
Let me alone!

MAN:
You haven't understood, gentlemen, that I cannot lose!

ALLAN:
(jesting) Yes, yes, I've understood! Let's see the cards.

CLAIRELI:
And with all your money, you married the one you loved?

MAN:
No, madame, as for me, who never thought of a thing, I understood that day that I was damned! When one is damned, one no longer thinks of marrying an angel!

CLAIRELI:
(rising) What are you thinking of? You needn't call the devil!

(passionately) As for me, I am for those who know what they want!

ALLAN:
Let's see the cards.

MATHIS:
Allan, don't do it.

MATHIEU:
You're wrong! No, don't do this!

MAN:
Cure me — I have done everything to be cured.

ALLAN:
You haven't played cards with me. Is it a long while since you played?

MAN:
(sitting down, looking at the cards that Allan has spread on the table) Since that period, never, after which I buried myself here — never. Why did you come with cards?

ALLAN:
(gathering the cards) What shall we play?

MAN:
(presenting the billfold where he arranged the

envelopes on the table) What you will. I bet you immediately all that's in this billfold — I will play you after that all the hands that you like!

ALLAN:
That'll work.

(turning towards his friends) Are we all of the party?

MATHIS:
No! No! As for me, I am not in!

MATHIEU:
Me neither!

CLAIRELI:
As for me, I'm in!

MATHIS:
No, indeed, I don't wish it.

CLAIRELI:
So be it.

MAN:
Ah, gentlemen! Now, I insist on silence.

ALLAN:
Who first? To the first king!

(he deals the cards) There! Yours!

MAN:
You see already — the first king!

ALLAN:
Eh! That one doesn't count! Your deal.

(he passes him the cards) I've already done everything to lose and it never happens to me.

MAN:
(after having tapped the cards) Cut.

(Allan cuts, the Man deals.)

ALLAN:
(looking at the cards) I draw.

MAN:
No, play, sir.

CLAIRELI:
(who looks at the man's play) What? You are playing that?

MAN:
Why, yes, madame. You see that I am doing everything necessary to lose!

ALLAN:
(playing) You will get there! The king! And I take it.

(the man plays, Allan gathers the hand and deals again) Trump — hearts.

MAN:
(playing) There.

ALLAN:
Why, is all you have clubs?

(playing) Diamonds.

MAN:
(playing) That's good!

ALLAN:
And there! With the point of refusal I take three! And I still have a small trump! Well, why, say! That's not going very badly! Be careful of your ten thousand, my dear host!

CLAIRELI:
The wood of Misère is going to go away!

(Man, without replying, wipes his face.)

ALLAN:
(after having lost, The Man cuts, Allan deals the cards) Trumps, diamonds.

MAN:
(happily and jubilant) This time I don't have it.

ALLAN:
(taking it) Diamonds, I take! Huh! Your hope is reviving?

(playing) I'm coming into colors.

MAN:
(uneasily) Ah! I've got it — I'm obliged to take it.

(The Man pulls in the cards, then plays hesitantly.)

ALLAN:
(playing) Don't tremble! I take and trump!

MATHIEU:
(behind Allan, in a triumphant tone) Trump! Trump and trump again! And pass diamonds!

(to man) Ah! This time! You are there — you are indeed there! That makes five points!

ALLAN:
(after having played his cards in the sequence cried out by Mathieu) I've won, sir!

MAN:
(terrified, exhausted with joy) It's not possi-

ble! Not possible!

(looking at his adversary's hand) Then —
then — My God! — I've lost!

ALLAN:
Damn! It seems that way!

(giving him an amicable pat on the shoulder)
You see, it's not necessary to believe everything the devil says.

(At this moment the wind begins its song
over again, more lugubriously)

MAN:
(trembling with joy, taking his billfold from
the table and opens it) Gentlemen! Gentlemen! Be — be blessed! Take them! Take the
agreed ten thousand francs!

(so saying, he looks in the billfold for the ten
thousand francs, and the others worriedly like
him, seeing that he has nothing in his billfold,
for they also saw him put the ten thousand in

it) But — where are they? Where are they?

(more forcefully) Where are they? But, you saw them plainly, the rest of you?

ALL:
(stupefied, terrified) Yes! Yes! We saw them! They were there! You put them there!

MAN:
(wildly) There! There! I put them there!

(he searches) But search me! Search me, will you?

(Claireli searches the billfold.)

CLAIRELI:
(replacing the billfold) Nothing!

MAN:
(haggard) I gambled with what was in the billfold and there is nothing in the billfold!

(three rough knocks on the door, in a trembling voice) Who is there?

GUILLAUME:
(outside) It's me, Guillaume!

(The man goes to open.)

MAN:
What is it you want?

GUILLAUME:
(coming forward) I beg your pardon, gentle-men — I thought I'd given you ten thousand francs just now.

MATHIEU:
(terrified) Yes, indeed!

GUILLAUME:
Probably not, since I still have them! I must have taken them from their envelope without paying attention.

MATHIS:
(pointing to the man) This gentlemen had

gathered them!

MAN:
When did you become aware of it?

GUILLAUME:
In passing in front of the Grande Marnière — a gust of wind opened my bag. I put my hand in to prevent the papers from blowing away — I felt the ten thousand! I would not have been more astonished if they had returned by themselves all alone and if the wind had brought them to me — and then I said to myself — Finally, here they are!

(opening his bag)

CLAIRELI:
Indeed, this is extraordinary.

ALLAN:
Yes — I'd really thought —

(Mathieu and Mathis consider Guillaume with shock.)

GUILLAUME:
(after having given the ten bills to the Man) There they are — and there's no error — this time I'm not bringing them back! Goodnight, everybody. Decidedly, master, I am sleeping here — I'll get up as early as I can in the morning.

(Guillaume leaves by the door to the office.)

MAN:
(as if hypnotized by the bills) Let's go to play now. We were playing with nothing. Here's the money. The ten thousand francs to who-ever wins, and hell beneath the path.

ALLAN:
Yours.

MAN:
Cards!

ALLAN:
Play!

MAN:
(spreading the cards) Ah! I cannot toss them this time! The king and four trumps! That makes three for me.

(he takes the trick, deals frenetically and returns the king) The king! That gives me four (showing his hand) and the point — that gives me five! And it's always like this! Always! Always!

(he throws the cards in the fire) Ah! Let's — let's burn the cards!

(haggard, fists in his hair, he drags himself almost to the stairway, repeating) Why — did you come with cards! Why did — you come with cards? Why did you come with cards?

(The Man vanishes. Mathis and Mathieu are stunned, the two others very affected.)

MATHIS:
Ah! Why, as for me, I cannot stay a moment longer in this house.

(Violent storm, thunderclap.)

ALLAN:
Oh! He is completely mad!

MATHIEU:
It is possible.

MATHIS:
While waiting, let's go to our rooms.

CLAIRELI:
But we were to spend the night playing here.

MATHIS:
(brutally) Tomorrow morning, we must rise very early, and then, if there's a good bed, we will be better than here.

ALLAN:
(somberly) No, I am staying here.

MATHIS:
(to Claireli) Go up!

CLAIRELI:

No one's going to sleep now, after such a story. Better to remain here!

MATHIS:

(furious, leaves, slamming the door) No indeed, no, indeed, come —

CLAIRELI:

I'll follow you.

(Mathis and Mathieu leave.)

ALLAN:

Go away, Claireli!

CLAIRELI:

(in a low voice) Ah! I don't want to leave you this evening; I'm afraid of joining him.

ALLAN:

It's necessary, my love.

CLAIRELI:

Silence! But it's your fault! We, too, we have

had the devil with us — But men don't know what they want! Look at him who prayed to the devil to win: he begs God now to lose! And, you yourself, if you knew what you wanted — Mathis won't wait for me tonight.

ALLAN:
Ah! I wasn't thinking of that.

MATHIS:
(in the corridor, then at the door) Well? Aren't you coming?

CLAIRELI:
Yes —

(calmly) I was asking Allan if it didn't bother him being left like this — all alone — face to face with the devil.

(she leaves laughing)

MATHIS:
Have a good night, Allan.

(Only one lamp feebly lights the stage, for Mama Appenzel has come in the meantime to extinguish the other lamp on the table.)

ALLAN:
Face to face with the devil!

(he looks around him as if he were awakening from a bad dream. He goes to a window and pushes the blinds. Soon a burst of blue moonlight illuminates the stage. He leans suddenly out the window) What solitude! What a terrible desert!

(suddenly, he hastily shuts the blinds and turns) Heavens! A vulture — perhaps the bird the old boy was speaking about.

(then he comes back) Well, what! What's wrong with me?

(turning to the window and looking out) He's still there — motionless on his perch — like a bronze bird. It's true, he's impressive enough.

(going to the door with the cross) This story of the old man is coming back to me. Ah! The door, the famous door!

(saying this he looks at door, taps it, shakes it) It holds well! It's not for me that it will open all by itself.

(at this moment the door with the cross releases and slowly opens, revealing a large mirror, Allan cannot keep himself from recoiling) Ah! Ah! The famous mirror! The cupboard mirror. Hello, Allan! You don't have a very good appearance, my lad. Let's see the cupboard now.

(he makes an effort to open the cupboard) If the devil pulls on his side, this can last a long while.

(the mirror gives way in the same manner the door with cross did) Ah!

(looking in the cupboard) Well, why, there's a very honest cupboard.

(he takes the lamp and lights the interior of the cupboard) Books — heavens! And here — here, letters graven in the scorched wood.

(raises the lamp) "You will win!" The old boy didn't dream it! Bah! A fantastic old inscription which upset his mind.

(these words are spoken with a certain hesitancy because Allan is more and more affected. Now, he looks at the books in the cupboard, he takes one and shuts the cupboard) Ah! Ah! And, for a book, that of the sorcerer of Jura!

(places the lamp on some furniture, opens the book and says) Good heavens! Why, this is curious.

(reading) "When one sincerely wants to see the devil, you have only to call him: he'll come! But you must call him with all your heart."

(he reads a few moments in silence, then

shutting the book, and striking his hand on the table) All the same, it's curious, that bird here — and the other one — down there. Still, with a good rifle shot —

(taking his rifle) Yes, but I — as for me, I am certain to miss — as Mathis says — I always forget to aim properly.

(furious, suddenly) Ah! That Mathis! What a brute! Claireli is right — when he kisses her in front of me.

(he grasps his rifle like a hunter shooting from cover) There are moments when I wish — (feverishly) I wish —

(at this moment the mirror makes a slight noise and Allan turns his head) The cupboard is going to open.

(he slowly rests the rifle on the table and after a few steps turns toward the mirror, repeating) What is it I want?

(the reflection comes out of the mirror) What is it I want?

(seeing The Other One)

(in a dull, choked voice) Who are you? What do you want? Where are you coming from? Are you the devil?

(they lean towards each other, face to face, then recoil, making motions that are identical but opposite as if they were symmetric reflections of each other) You frighten me — What are you bringing me? Will?

(they both slowly kiss the handle of the rifle) Will! Everything is in it. And he will never make fun of me any more! Ever! Right? What? What did you say? One can always think that a rifle isn't loaded! You are the devil or the bottom of my thought? Accident! You said "Accident!" Don't go — don't go yet! When you are there I feel so powerful! The true Allan is you! I'm afraid of day which will chase away your shadow! It's really you who left the mirror just now? Where are you now? Where are you?

(The Other One returns into the mirror. Allan rushes towards him but the moment he touches the mirror it breaks and he falls into a faint as the reflection vanishes.)

CURTAIN

ACT II

Same set, darkness.

Allan is stretched at the foot of the mirror. Mathis and Mathieu enter, already prepared to leave, with bandoleros and rifles.

MATHIEU:
Allan!

(Mathieu comes forward. He goes to the window and opens it. Beautiful dawn. Mathis goes to the door, pulls back the bolt and opens it.)

BOTH:
(noticing Allan at the foot of the mirror) Ah!

(they rush to him) What's happened to him?

(They raise Allan and take him to the arm-chair.)

MATHIEU:
And the devil's door is open!

MATHIS:
I said some misfortune would happen to us!

(They place Allan in the armchair. Allan utters a sigh.)

MATHIEU:
He's sighing! He must be coming back from a long distance.

MATHIS:
(shaking his head) Farther perhaps than you may think.

(They watch him awaken with anxious curiosity.)

ALLAN:
(coming out of his torpor) What's this?

(recognizing Mathis) Mathis! You! You! Ah! You!

(He shakes his hand effusively.)

MATHIS:
We found you stretched there at the foot of the mirror. No doubt you saw the evil one, huh?

ALLAN:
(speechless) Ah! A nightmare! An abominable dream! What! Really! You found me at the foot of the mirror?

MATHIEU:
Hell yes, fainted!

ALLAN:
(stupidly) Yes! Yes! I remember — now — I wanted to do evil— I opened the door with the cross — and then —

MATHIEU AND MATHIS:
And then?

ALLAN:
And then, I was taken by a vertigo! Bang! That's it — and I had a dream — a dream.

(Allan rises and shakes Mathis' hands.)

MATHIS:
What's got into him?

ALLAN:
(more and more tenderly) My dear, good, old comrade! I love you a lot, you know!

MATHIS:
I've never doubted it.

ALLAN:
How stupid, dreams! (looking to the right and the left) How stupid!

MATHIEU:
What are you looking for?

ALLAN:
My rifle!

MATHIS:
(passing the rifle to Allan) There's your rifle.

ALLAN:
(feverishly) Give it to me! Give it to me!

(he tips it open) Ah! — it's not loaded! It's not loaded!

(whistling down the barrel) It's not loaded!

MATHIEU:
Damnation! Why do you expect it to be loaded?

ALLAN:
(gaily) He lied, the devil!

MATHIS:
Could you have seen him, too?

ALLAN:
Yes, I saw him! Quite certainly I saw him! Ah! Gang! What a dream! I have to tell you about it.

CLAIRELI:
(in the wings) Allan! Mathis!

ALLAN:
Heavens! Claireli's voice — She's gone already?

(he places his rifle near the stairway.)

MATHIS:
Yes — the door of our room gives directly on the plateau — she was the first one up.

CLAIRELI:
(in the wings) Why, will you come on! Come see the rising of the sun! If you knew how beautiful it is!

MATHIS:
You will tell us your tale later.

(He leaves. All leave.)

VOICES FROM OUTSIDE
Ah! It's magnificent! Magnificent!

(Mama Appenzel enters from the office door and notices immediately that the door with the cross is open.)

MAMA:
Ah! Who did that? Who dared to touch it?

(She places the cups and the pot of milk that she has under her arm on the table.)

GUILLAUME:
(above on the stairs) What's wrong?

MAMA:
They opened the door and the mirror is broken.

GUILLAUME:
(coming down) Really! The mirror is broken! That's a sign of bad luck! Yes, where are all

of them? The master doesn't want to see them! I must help them bring their traps to the farm and then, past the Grande Marnière, goodbye! He doesn't want any accident to happen to them! But they've flown the coop! Ah! There's the bag!

(he places the game bags over his shoulder) And then the rifles!

(he puts Allan's rifle in the bandolier, the only rifle that remains in the house because Mathis and Mathieu have taken theirs with them) There cannot be anything to it, no!

(he heads toward the exit door) All the same.

(looking at the door with the cross) Why did they touch that door there!

MAMA:
If the master sees that! That's going to give him a turn again!

GUILLAUME:
(at the door) Bah! I am going to be back soon to patch the door up for you.

MAMA:
(placing her wood on the table) So much the better! Because, as for me, I don't dare touch it! Ask them if they want to take a bowl of milk before leaving!

GUILLAUME:
Are you thinking? Especially, don't keep them.

(Guillaume leaves.)

MAMA:
(looking at the door with the cross) The pagans!

GUILLAUME:
(reappearing at the window) Ah! Mother! The damned vulture is there.

(Guillaume disappears.)

MAMA:
(running to the window) The damned vulture!
Well, leave him alone, let him be! You hear,
Guillaume!?

MAN'S VOICE:
(from his apartment) Guillaume! Guillaume!

MAMA: (at the window) Hurry, Guillaume,
the master's calling you.

ALLAN:
(entering, followed by Claireli, gaily) Yes,
indeed! Yes, indeed! Hello, Mama.

(giving a piece of gold to her) Here, that's for
the mirror!

CLAIRELI:
(looking toward the mirror) Ah! Tell me
about that!

MATHIEU:
He'll tell us on the way

MAMA:
A little warm milk, my little lady?

CLAIRELI:
That cannot be refused.

MATHIS:
Well, quickly then!

(Meanwhile, Guillaume returns through the back; the old woman makes a sign of the head that he should go to the Man's apartment.)

MAMA:
He's calling you.

(She pours milk for Claireli.)

GUILLAUME:
(placing the rifle in the corner, exactly where he took it from) I'm going there!

(Guillaume hastily mounts the stairway. Busy, the hunters have not paid any attention to Guillaume, and Allan hasn't even noticed him.)

ALLAN:
(responding immediately to the old woman's question) Why, as for me, I will take a little milk, too.

MATHIEU:
Ah! This will never end!

ALLAN:
(drinking) We cannot leave without thanking our host.

MATHIS:
The order will be taken — you are not going to wake him up, perhaps.

CLAIRELI:
(to Allan, standing, drinking in little gulps) Then, you saw the devil? Is he handsome?

ALLAN:
He resembles me, Claireli.

CLAIRELI:

That's not bad! And what did you say to each other?

MATHIEU:

Ah! We will speak of that outside.

MATHIS:

Yes, he will tell us his story en route! And, hurrying a bit, we might still meet the stag at the awakening of Mount Huon.

ALLAN:

(placing his bowl down, taking his rifle, banteringly) Then, let's go again to the slaughter!

MATHIS:

(by the door, to Allan) Oh! As for you, don't forget to load!

ALLAN:

Ah! You are starting again! Well, here, I am going to finish my tale immediately. In my dream, as you've just spoken to me of it again, my loading — I aimed at you.

MATHIS:
So that's why you looked right away to see if your rifle wasn't loaded!

ALLAN:
Exactly! And I said to you: "Son of William Tell, do you want me to croak you?"

(aiming) Right eye or left eye!

MATHIS:
Left eye!

(Allan leans on the trigger, the gun fires, Mathis falls in a heap. The two men rush to Mathis. Allan is almost mad.)

ALLAN:
I killed him!

MATHIEU:
Mathis! Mathis!

(Both are on their knees the body of Mathis.)

GUILLAUME:
(running in, coming down the stairs like a madman) A misfortune! A misfortune! The rifle!

(He hurls himself on Mathis' body.)

ALLAN:
(taking the body in his arms) What have I done? Mathis! My old comrade!

MATHIEU:
He is dead!

ALLAN:
(who has leaned his head on Mathis' breast in the anguished silence, rises and reveals a face of the damned) Dead!

CLAIRELI:
(who was leaning in a pose of shock on the table, repeats, eyes enlarged by horror, looking at Allan meaningfully) Dead!

ALLAN:
(finishing getting up, haggard) Who loaded the gun?

(Allan turns toward the door with the cross.)

GUILLAUME:
(still on his knees, arms to heaven) It was me! It was me!

ALLAN:
You?

GUILLAUME:
Yes, me.

ALLAN:
But, why?

GUILLAUME:
There was a vulture; I wanted to shoot it. I saw your rifle, I loaded it. At that moment, they called me.

ALLAN:
(disregarding a gesture by Guillaume, and looking towards the Armoire) No! No! I know quite well, I do, I know who loaded the rifle.

(leaning an arm on the ground with a convulsive gesture) Why, he even left a cartridge!

(Guillaume and Claireli rush to Allan.)

GUILLAUME:
What is it you want to do now? What is it you want to do now?

CLAIRELI:
This is enough of a misfortune.

(Guillaume wrests the rifle from Allan.)

ALLAN:
(pushing Claireli away who has helped Guillaume to disarm him) Ah! You, Claireli. I don't know you! I don't know you! It's you who killed him!

CLAIRELI:
Me!

ALLAN:
(completely delirious) Yes, you! You! You killed my friend! It's you who put death into the rifle. It's you who sent the Other One to me last night! It's you! May I never see you again! Never! Never!

MAN:
(appearing at the height of the stairs with a ghastly voice) Why was that door touched?

(During these last words, the voice of the old woman is heard repeating "What a misfortune! What a misfortune!" and the quaking of Mathieu who leaning over the body keeps calling lugubriously, "Mathis! Mathis! Mathis!")

CURTAIN

ABOUT FRANK J. MORLOCK

FRANK J. MORLOCK has written and translated many plays since retiring from the legal profession in 1992. His translations have also appeared on Project Gutenberg, the Alexandre Dumas Père web page, Literature in the Age of Napoléon, Infinite Artistries.com, and Munsey's (formerly Blackmask). In 2006 he received an award from the North American Jules Verne Society for his translations of Verne's plays. He lives and works in México.